MINNESOTA'S VIKINGS

The Scrambler

and the

Purple Gang

MINNESOTA'S VIKINGS
The Scrambler and the Purple Gang

by Bob Rubin

Photography by Malcolm Emmons/
John and Vernon Biever

A Stuart L. Daniels Book

PRENTICE-HALL, INC.
Englewood Cliffs, New Jersey

MINNESOTA'S VIKINGS
The Scrambler and the Purple Gang

by Bob Rubin

Copyright © 1973 by
The Stuart L. Daniels Company, Inc.

Published by Prentice-Hall, Inc.
Englewood Cliffs, New Jersey

Printed in the United States of America • T
Prentice-Hall International, Inc., London
Prentice-Hall of Australia, Pty. Ltd., Sydney
Prentice-Hall of Canada, Ltd., Toronto
Prentice-Hall of India Private Ltd., New Delhi
Prentice-Hall of Japan, Inc., Tokyo

Library of Congress Catalog Card Number: 73-7224

ISBN: 0-13-584565-3 (paperbound)

ISBN: 0-13-584573-4 (hardbound)

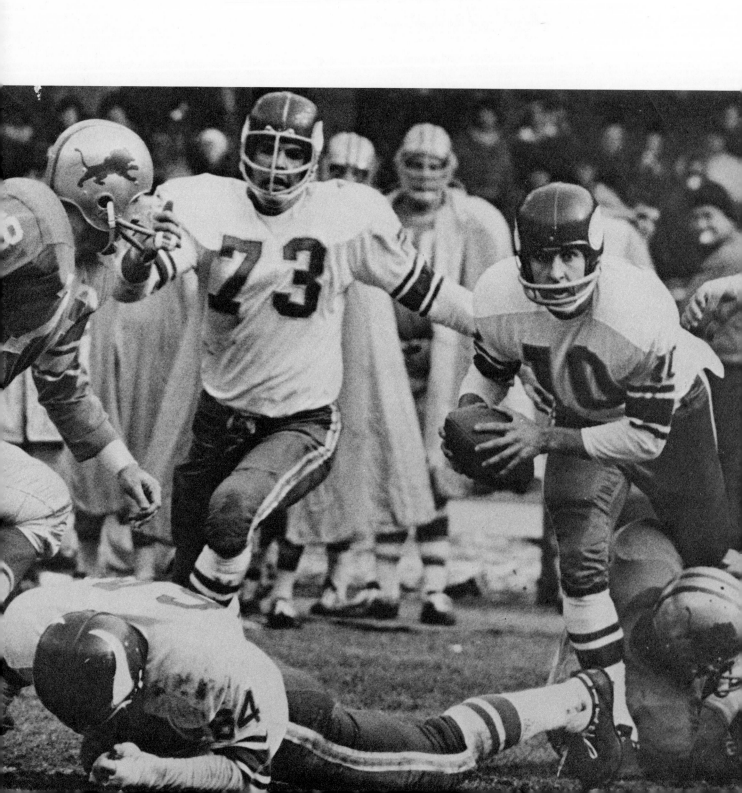

football –
backwoods style

It was July 1961, in Bemidji, Minnesota, and amidst the thick tamarack groves that surround Bemidji State College, the Minnesota Vikings, a brand new football team which had just been awarded a franchise by the National Football League, was struggling to be born.

In exchange for its $600,000 entrance fee, the Vikings had been given an assorted group of thirty-six professional players spun off from the NFL's existing franchises. There were others who turned up for that first organizational day, among them a 320-pound bartender from Ishpeming, Michigan, whose football knowledge had been gleaned from a paperback football annual that protruded from his back pocket, a six-foot-nine Swede who could barely make the quarter mile to the practice field, and other ambitious misfits.

his early picture illustrates how Viking ran Tarkenton acquired the appellation Scrambler," as he steps over a fallen Lion fender.

The picture, however, was not all glum. Among the draftees in that first camp were a few nuggets of gold—Fran Tarkenton, a bright, slick, confident young quarterback, Tommy Mason, a swift, hard-running back, and Rip Hawkins, a promising middle linebacker.

Some of the veterans handed to the fledgling Vikings by the older NFL teams were also to prove their worth. There was former 49ers' running back Hugh McElhenny, no longer a youth but still superb in the open field, and Grady Alderman, a young offensive tackle discarded by the Detroit Lions; but five good players do not make a football team, so the Vikings had to carefully survey all the hardy souls who showed up ambitious to play football.

It was enough to make coach Norm Van Brocklin, an All-Pro quarterback who had led the Philadelphia Eagles to the NFL Championship the season before, wonder if he shouldn't have delayed his retirement as a player and debut as a coach until, oh, say, until he had a team to work with. He looked over his charges, thought for a minute, spat on the ground and said, "Stiffs. They gave me thirty-six stiffs for a football team."

Those early, awkward, ill-matched Vikings seemed a million light years away from championship contention. Surprisingly, it took only eight years for the Minnesota team to come close to winning football's greatest prize, the Super Bowl.

In this Nov. 28, 1969, action against St. Louis, Joe Kapp is in full command of his team as he gets good protection by staying in a well-fortified pocket.

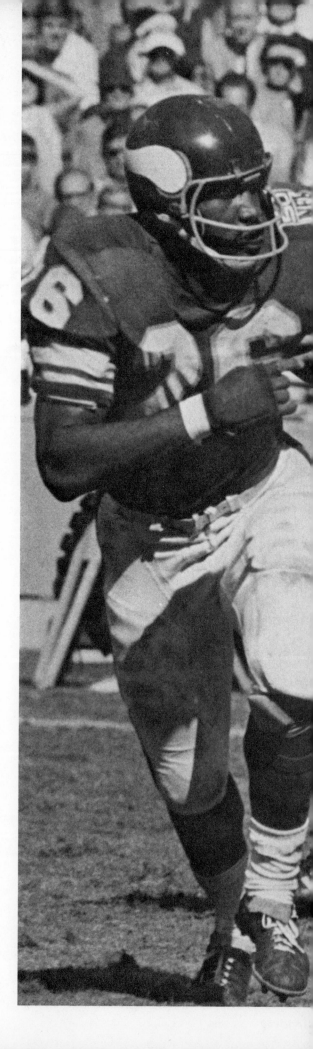

Fred Cox is a consistent kicker and a high scorer, but occasionally he fakes a kick

. . . and placekicker Paul Krause is called upon to perform other duties, such as running with the ball.

Kansas City runner Wendell Hayes isn't going anywhere as four Viking defenders move in quickly.

formative years

On a balmy fall day in 1959, while a large crowd assembled in Metropolitan Stadium in Bloomington, Minnesota, to watch the New York Giants trounce the St. Louis Cardinals, two almost simultaneous events were determining the future of major league football in Minneapolis-St. Paul. The avid desire of the Twin Cities' citizens for their own football team had been emphasized by the fact that local business interests had offered quite a large sum to the Cardinals to play that day as well as the previous week.

Just as Giant quarterback Charlie Conerly was throwing his last touchdown pass of the day, the contents were released of a telegram sent to Charles Johnson, sports editor of the *Minneapolis Star* and *Tribune,* by the Chicago Bears' owner, George Halas, who was then chairman of the NFL's expansion committee. It said, in effect, that the National Football League was on the verge of offering a franchise to Minneapolis-St. Paul.

On that very day, Texas oil tycoons Lamar Hunt and Bud Adams, along with New York sportscaster Harry Wismer and former Notre Dame coach Frank Leahy, who represented Barron Hilton of the hotel family, were meeting with three local business executives, Max Winter, Bill Boyer and H. P. Skoglund at the Pick-Nicollet Hotel in Minneapolis. The first group was in the process of forming the American Football League, and the Minneapolis-St. Paul group was discussing a franchise for their city.

In actuality, the Minnesotans would have preferred an NFL franchise, but since the established league was still debating the merits of the Twin Cities against offers from other localities, the negotiations with the AFL founders served a double purpose: to euchre the NFL into granting a franchise and, if that failed, at least to provide the football-hungry cities with a major-league team.

Early in 1960, the three would-be owners joined forces with Bernard Ridder, whose newspaper interests included the *St. Paul Dispatch* and *Pioneer Press,* and Ole Haugsrud, who was an essential key to an NFL franchise. Haugsrud had been the owner of the NFL's Eskimos and had what amounted to a first option if and when a Minnesota franchise was reactivated.

At its annual winter meeting in Miami in 1960, the National Football League, after voting to make Pete Rozelle its new commissioner and granting a Dallas franchise to the Murchisons of oil riches, also approved the Minneapolis-St. Paul bid for NFL membership. The Minnesota team was to begin play in the fall of 1961.

Jeff Siemon, an All-American at Stanford, has one of the brightest futures of any young linebacker in the pros.

Bob Berry, brought back to Minnesota from Atlanta, where he served as the Falcons' starting quarterback, is now the backup to Fran Tarkenton.

The total investment was a $600,000 initial payment, to be followed by a later payment of $400,000. By 1973, the franchise was worth an estimated $20,000,000.

Stock ownership of the new club was divided 60 percent to the Winter-Boyer-Skoglund Minneapolis group, 30 percent to the Ridders of St. Paul and 10 percent to Ole Haugsrud. This is still the Vikings' basic ownership setup. Though each charter owner has sold some stock, the original group retains exclusive voting rights. Ridder is chairman of the board; Winter is president; Boyer, vice-president; Haugsrud, secretary; and Skoglund, treasurer.

Certain conditions stipulated by the league were that Metropolitan Stadium was to be enlarged to 40,000 seats, and there would have to be 25,000 season-ticket sales by the opening game.

Ignoring indignant howls of treason and threats of legal action from the disappointed AFL brass, the Minnesota team prepared to set up shop. Commissioner Pete Rozelle suggested, "You've got a chance to look at the college spring practices this year [1960], looking toward your first draft in the fall. You need a scout."

Rozelle then recommended Joe Thomas, a Los Angeles Rams assistant coach when Rozelle was general manager, as a scout for the new team.

A Coach Is Found

After considering such men as Sid Gillman, coach of the AFL San Diego Chargers, Nick Skorich, assistant coach of the Philadelphia Eagles, Mike Nixon, a Washington Redskins assistant, Ara Parseghian, coach of Northwestern University, Otto Graham, former Cleveland Browns quarterback, Bud Grant, coach of the Winnipeg team in the Canadian league, they finally settled on Norm Van Brocklin, just finishing his great career with the Philadelphia Eagles.

spite his many years as a pro, Bill Brown
oves with the strength and speed of a
unger man.

Van Brocklin was and is a difficult man to portray. Intelligent, impulsive, but most of all, demanding. He brought to the Vikings his own massive ego and boundless self-confidence, with expectations of his team that were not always to be fulfilled. When pleased, he was happy and joking—but Van Brocklin is probably more remembered for his explosive bursts of fury that erupted when he was angry. Tantrums were frequent and arguments with teammates abounded; there was also a history of fights with newsmen. But off the field he was filled with good humor and anecdotes—"a merry, needling leprechaun in the clubhouse or at the bar," as Viking historian Jim Klobuchar has put it.

Van Brocklin and Tarkenton

The Vikings' first year with Van Brocklin went as one might have expected—they completed 1961 with a 3–11 record. The next year was worse, 2–11–1, and 1963 produced a 5–8–1 ending. Though the games weren't very good in those early years, they certainly weren't boring, and the Vikings began to develop a kind of loose togetherness, an odd combination of toughness and zaniness that was a direct reflection of their two leaders, Van Brocklin and Fran Tarkenton. Occasionally, even the tough guy succumbed and did something flaky, like the time after a particularly bad 1961 beating at the hands of San Francisco, when he told his startled and grateful athletes, "Let's forget the Tuesday practice and go drink beer." But mostly he was just tough.

A look into the past—Fran Tarkenton and coach Norm Van Brocklin back in the early 1960s.

Early Highlights

Those early Vikings infuriated the more orthodox clubs in the league on the few occasions that they beat them. One such incident involved the Chicago Bears' George Halas, probably the best-known establishment figure in pro football. His big, bad Bears were the first regular-season opponents in Viking history . . . and their first victims.

18

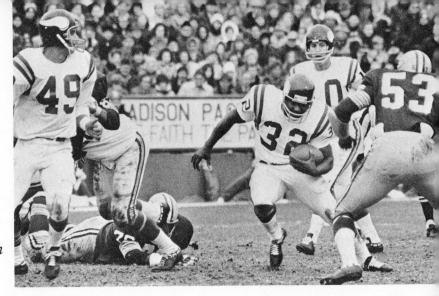

Oscar Reed sidesteps Fred Carr of Green Bay.

The Vikings' offensive line was a primary factor in their 1969 NFL title victory.

That it wasn't going to be their day became apparent when the snap for their punt sailed into the Metropolitan Stadium stands. Midway through the second quarter, Tarkenton replaced Shaw at quarterback, for good, as it turned out. Within three minutes he had thrown his first NFL touchdown pass. He added numbers two and three in the third period and number four in the final quarter. Just for added measure, he also ran for a score before the final gun.

The score: Vikings 37, Bears 13.

The neophyte fans were not nearly so awed by the dimensions of the upset as was the visiting press. "Look at them" said a writer from Baltimore, observing the applauding fans. "They really don't know the enormity of this. It's like Luxembourg beating the Kaiser's army. Oh Lord, Lord. I would hate to be the Bears when Halas gets to them."

Surprisingly, Halas said nothing in the Bears' dressing room. He said nothing on the ride to the airport or during the boarding. It was not until his fallen warriors were seated and on their way back to Chicago that the crusty old man evaluated their performance.

It was succinct. Roared Halas: "You Goddamned pussies!" Then he sat down.

The next great moment in Viking history came three years later, in 1964, when they beat the Green Bay Packers for the first time.

If there was anyone more authoritarian or establishment than George Halas, it was Green Bay's Vince Lombardi, whose approach to the game was based on meticulous planning and execution, not exactly the Vikings' style in those days. With less than a minute to play, the Packers led by two points and had the Vikings down to a fourth-and-twenty-two prayer on their own thirty-six-yard line. It seemed likely that planning and execution had won another one.

In the late 1960s, quarterback Joe Kapp was the talk of Minnesota.

Tarkenton surveyed the Packers' defense—seven men spread out as far as forty yards downfield. The quarterback concluded that they were looking for the pass, and since there was no sense in calling a set play against such as array, he told the huddle, "Everyone eligible go deep." If he could run around long enough, maybe something would happen.

Tarkenton went into his scrambling act and avoided the Packer defense. He threw to Tom Ball, who was near the Packers' twenty-yard line. Just as Hall was about to catch the ball, end Gordie Smith grabbed it. From this point, Fred Cox kicked a field goal and the Vikings had their one-point victory.

A Slow Start

Such successes were few and far between, as the club's record in those early years clearly shows. The victory over the Packers was the highlight of their first winning season, 8–5–1, but instead of marking the start of an ascent to the top, it proved a false harbinger of spring. The Vikings slipped back to 7–7 in 1965 and 4–9–1 in 1966, a season that ended with Tarkenton demanding to be traded.

The relationship between Van Brocklin and Tarkenton had become virtually nonexistent by the end of '66. The fiery coach had come to believe that Tarkenton's scrambling ways not only would not win a championship but that they reflected a basic selfishness on the quarterback's part, a desire to create headlines at the expense of his teammates and his team. Tarkenton respected and still respects Van Brocklin's undeniably great football mind, but had for years silently been growing tired of his coach's mercurial ups and downs and his public abuse of his players, and he understandably bridled at the suggestion that he was less than a 100-percent team man. When Van Brocklin publicly began to talk about trading his quarterback after the 1966 season ended, Tarkenton decided to beat him to the punch.

Green Bay's All-Pro runner John Brock-ington gets sandwiched between two Vik-ing defenders.

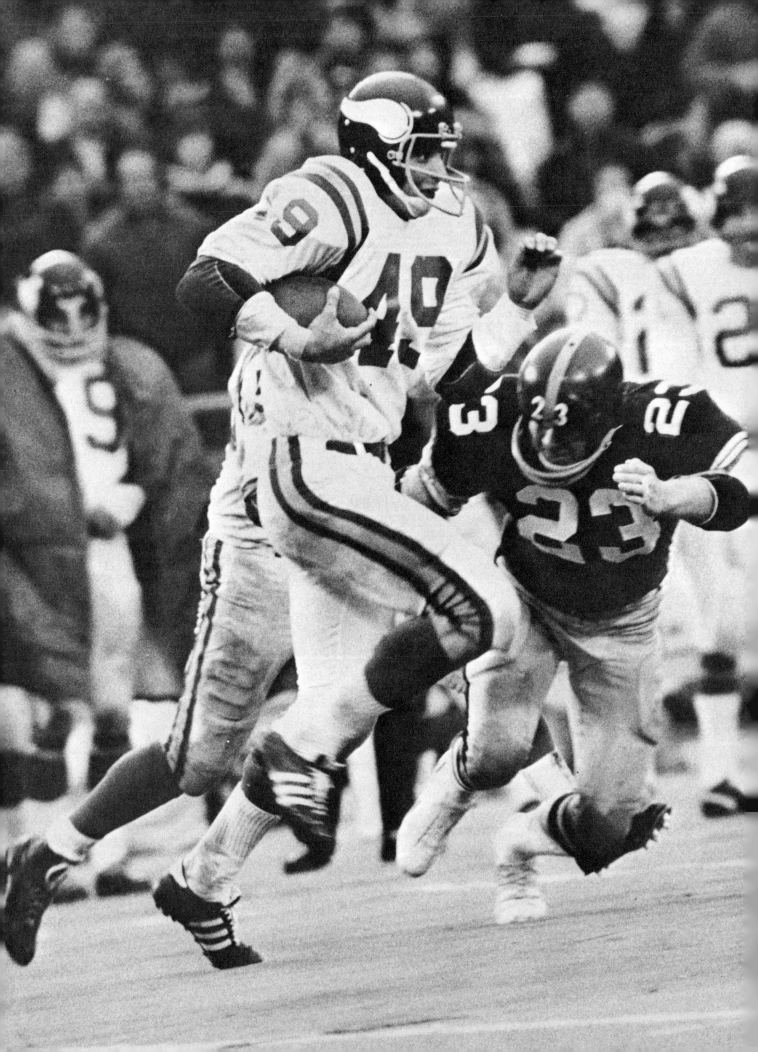

The following day, Van Brocklin resigned, frustrated with his inability to put the Vikings over the hump from mediocrity to championship status. He was bitterly disappointed with their poor showing in 1966, a distinct step backward from the 8–5–1 and 7–7 marks of the previous two years, and unhappy about petty squabbling within his coaching staff. He had quit in frustration for one day in 1965, but had been persuaded to come back. This time his mind couldn't be changed. "Maybe I'm just a pioneer-type coach, good with a new team. I don't think it's going to work anymore. I think I'd better get out."

So he resigned, and soon afterward became coach of the fledgling Atlanta Falcons.

Vikings' Ed Marinaro displays the same outstanding form against Pittsburgh that led him to record-breaking achievements at Cornell.

Building the Team

Despite the discouragement of the setbacks suffered in the 1965 and '66 seasons, the Vikings were slowly, at times almost imperceptibly, acquiring the players who would form the NFL power later in the decade.

Bert Rose, former publicity director of the University of Washington and the Los Angeles Rams, had been hired as the Vikings' general manager. He was not the guiding force behind the acquisitions, however. Unable to get along with Van Brocklin and unloved by the club's ownership, he resigned early in 1964 and was replaced by Jim Finks. An ex-Pittsburgh Steeler and assistant coach at Notre Dame, Finks had been general manager of the Calgary Stampeders from 1958 until he replaced Rose. It was Jim Finks and Bud Grant, Van Brocklin's replacement, who deserve the lion's share of credit for the rise of the Vikings, though a number of players from championship clubs did join the team in the Rose-Van Brocklin era.

25

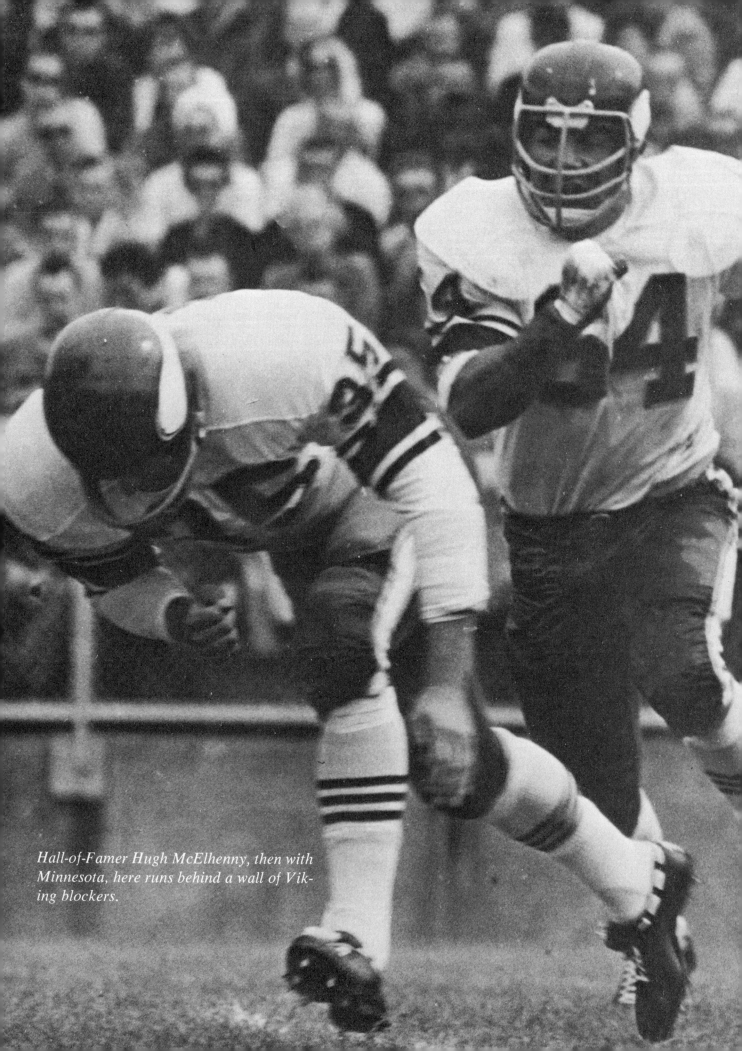

Hall-of-Famer Hugh McElhenny, then with Minnesota, here runs behind a wall of Viking blockers.

enter
bud grant

The year Bud Grant became coach was 1967, and it was that same year that the Vikings took a giant step from their humble beginnings at expansion toward becoming an established NFL power. Tarkenton was traded to the Giants for four draft choices: Clinton Jones, Bob Grim (ironically, the key Viking in the trade that brought Tarkenton back from New York), Ron Yary and Ed White, though Yary didn't join the club until 1968 and White until 1969. In addition, the Vikings also drafted Alan Page, Gene Washington, Bobby Bryant and John Beasley.

Coach Bud Grant is usually emphatic with his instructions. Quarterback Fran Tarkenton is the recipient of this lecture.

The pressure is on Tarkenton. Many feel that he must bring a championship to the Twin Cities.

Minnesota coach Bud Grant (left) and NFL Commissioner Pete Rozelle converse prior to Super Bowl V.

Cornerback Bobby Bryant (20) helps Paul Krause (22) intercept a pass as he holds back Green Bay's Carroll Dale.

In 1968, safety Charlie West, fullback Oscar Reed and quarterback Bob Lee joined Yary as draftees, Paul Krause came in a trade with Washington, and John Henderson and Wally Hilgenberg were claimed on waivers. Linebacker Noel Jenke and White were 1969 draftees, and in '70, guard John Ward, tight end Stu Voight and center John Zaunbrecker were taken in. The next year, tackle Jerry Patton was signed as a free agent, and running back Leo Hayden and safety Jeff Wright came in as draftees. Three players arrived via trades—tight end Bob Brown, cornerback Nate Wright and defensive end Doug Sutherland.

Fran Tarkenton and John Gilliam were the big acquisitions of 1972, along with the club's two top draft choices, middle linebacker Jeff Siemon of Stanford, an excellent prospect, and Ed Marinaro. Punter Mike Eischeid and wide receiver Leo Johnson also were obtained in trades with Kansas City and Chicago, respectively.

The Vital Acquisition

But no acquisition the Vikings ever made was more important than their choice of Harry Peter (Bud) Grant for coach.

Born in Superior, Wisconsin, Grant was the son of a fireman. A childhood case of polio left one leg shorter and thinner than the other, but by the time he was fifteen, at six-foot-three and weighing 180 pounds, he was ready to embark on distinguished high school careers in basketball, baseball and football, losing his boyhood limp in the process.

In Grant's freshman year of high school, he came into contact with football coach Harry Conley, "probably my most important influence," according to Grant. He was not to make that statement again until, having joined the Navy after high school, he played football for Paul Brown at the Great Lakes Naval Station. "If I had not

31

Fran Tarkenton ranked second in the
in passing statistics in 1972.

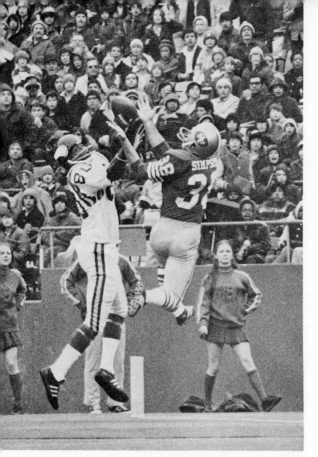

John Henderson, Viking wide receiver, and 49er safety Mike Simpson are open-handed and ready for a midair battle for the ball.

gone to Great Lakes and played under Paul Brown, I probably would have worked on an ore boat on Lake Superior the rest of my life," Grant says. "Through Brown, I saw a future in coaching. His outlook, his approach to football, impressed me. I knew then I'd have to go on to college."

Grant went to the University of Minnesota when he got out of the service and won nine varsity letters in baseball, basketball and football. In 1951 he was named the State of Minnesota's Athlete of the Half-Century.

The Philadelphia Eagles made him their number-one draft choice in 1949, but Grant elected to stay close to home and play basketball. He signed with the Minneapolis Lakers, but quit after two seasons and signed with the Eagles as defensive end. The next year, 1952, he switched to offense, and the following year he switched teams entirely, going to the Winnipeg Blue Bombers, where he played both offense and defense. When Winnipeg head coach Allie Sherman left to become a New York Giant assistant coach at the end of the 1956 season, the Blue Bombers offered Grant the job. He accepted. At twenty-nine, with no previous experience, he found himself a professional head coach.

Grant was an instant success. His first team won the Grey Cup, Canada's Super Bowl, four times in his first six years, and in his ten years as Winnipeg coach Grant compiled a record of 103–55–2. "I was lucky in Winnipeg," he says modestly. "I just hit the right winning cycle."

But Winnipeg also taught him a lesson that would manifest itself in spades with the Vikings. He saw nine of his regulars injured in 1964 and watched his team sink to a 1–14–1 record. "I never coached so hard in my life," he recalls. Eight of the nine injured players were from the defense. "It pointed out one thing to me," Grant said. "You don't win without defense....Offense sells tickets, but the defense wins the games."

e swarming Viking defense rushes in to o Green Bay runner Donny Anderson, o has just received the ball on a handoff m Packer quarterback Scott Hunter.

There was no question about who the Vikings wanted to replace Van Brocklin. They had let Grant get away from them once; this time they were determined to make him an offer he couldn't refuse. This time, however, Bud Grant *wanted* to come home. "I want to win in the National League," he explained. "I've won in the Canadian. . . . I love that country, but this country is my home, my land. I want to win in pro football in my land. It's that simple."

Fire and Ice

Grant asked for a three-year contract. Finks said the Vikings would give him more than that. "I don't want it," he replied. "If I can't establish something with the team in three years, I'm never going to do it."

In his leisure time, Grant is an ardent hunter and fisherman and a sly practical joker. But when he's involved with football . . . ice. "Van Brocklin hit a football team like a landslide," said one Viking lineman. "Grant comes at you like a glacier."

"I can't afford the luxury of emotions," Grant once said. "And I don't concern myself with things over which I have no control—the weather, the officiating, the bad breaks. I'm concerned about things I can do something about." That inner hardness encased in a mild-mannered, emotionless exterior became Grant's coaching trademark.

It didn't take long for everyone to begin to realize how serious—and tough—Bud Grant was. Speaking of his mania for discipline and precision, he once said, "It's an unconscious thing. We hope it will carry into the game, when real discipline is needed. You have to build this up in all your living habits, eating, sleeping, so that this is a natural step when you carry it on the field."

Winning—What It's All About

In Grant's mind, discipline produces winners, and winning is what it's all about. "I seek and employ players who help me win, because winning is what makes my profession a success. . . . I intend to win and I want my players to devote their desire and ambition to winning. I don't want nor will I tolerate a losing player. . . . If it's my neighbor, he goes."

Grant divides players into three categories. "First, you have the fellows who are 'squad men,'" he explains. "They are satisfied to make the team and get the benefits thereof. Regulars can be included in this category. Second, you have players who aren't quite satisfied with that. They want to do well. If they can individually do well, they are satisfied. The third type are the fellows who are only satisfied if the team wins. These are the real winners, and the team possessing the most number of these will win."

Grant, of course, concerned himself with more than just the outer reaches of discipline. The Vikings had a well-deserved reputation of fierce but, at times, foolish hitters, foolish in that it makes no sense to total a guy if it's going to cost you fifteen. Paradoxically, they also were known to be generous to a fault, giving up the ball in fumbles and interceptions with maddening regularity. One year they fumbled forty-five times. That's almost four per game. Grant decided these were areas that would be improved right away.

"We sat down and evaluated the entire picture," he said, recalling the days immediately following his appointment. "It was obvious we needed some new personnel, which means trading and drafting—and that takes time.

"So we decided to concentrate on areas where improvement could be immediate, like fumbles, interceptions and penalties. This doesn't just happen, either. We started by pointing out the values of the turnover and the elimination of mistakes."

Viking Jim Marshall has a handful of Mac-Arthur Lane's jersey as he attempts to pull him down from behind.

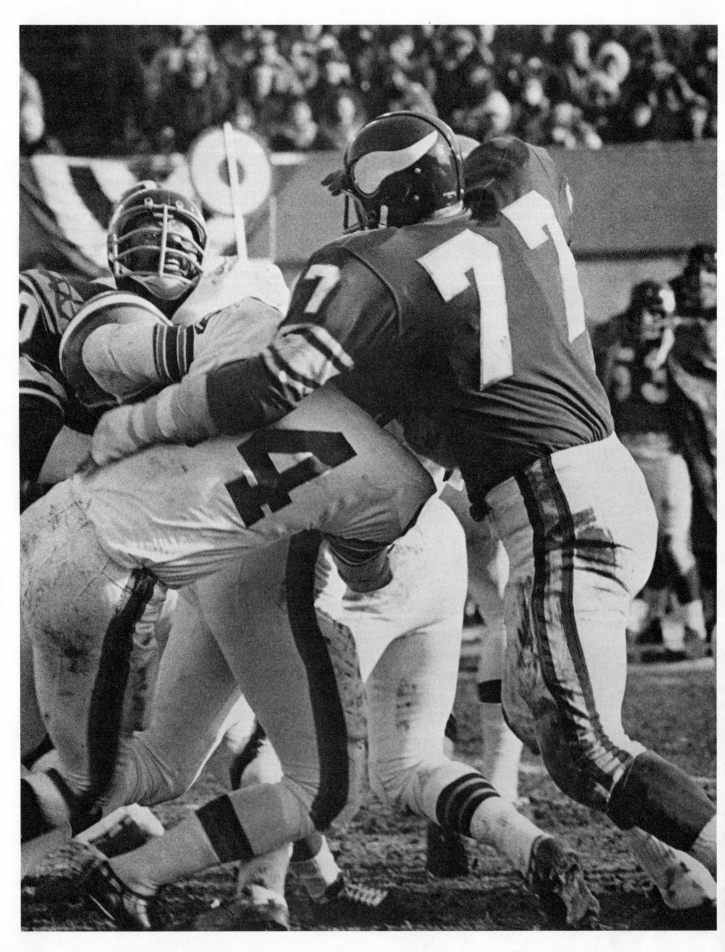

Coach Bud Grant and quarterback Joe Kapp, the key men responsible for Minnesota's 1969 NFL Championship, discuss strategy on the sidelines.

ry Larsen singlehandedly brings down eveland's great running back Leroy Kelly.

Slowly, grudgingly, the Vikings began to understand Grant. At first they called him the coach from Mars and went "beep beep" whenever he approached. They called the squad room "Grant's tomb." Gradually, however, they began to see certain Grant strengths. Recalls one Viking: "The guys started coming around to him because they saw that he was fair with the players. He gave every man a good shot. I think the thing that impressed them even more, maybe, was that he treated the guys decently. He never abused a man on the field or humiliated him. He would say things to individual players in meetings or on the field, but never in a way to make it sound like the guy had just evicted his mother."

The coach from Mars knew what his players were thinking when he first hit them with all those "Mickey Mouse" rules. He knew more than most people thought he did. When he took the job, he already had well-developed philosophies, in particular, about the 1967 Vikings.

He had a philosophy that he believed would build a winner. Now all he needed was a quarterback. The Vikings had gone to Canada for their general manager and their coach. They found their quarterback up north, too.

Quarterback Joe Kapp

Joe Kapp was sort of a Lee Trevino with muscles. Son of a Mexican-American mother and German-American father, he was, according to an admirer, "a guy who comes on like Pancho Villa and goes around like the Rhine—slowly but inevitably." Fun-loving, carefree, nomadic, pugnacious, fearless, awkward, charismatic—all describe the fascinating figure who would become the inartistic but undeniably effective leader of the Vikings through their finest years, before a salary impasse sent him packing to the Patriots after the 1969 season.

One of the University of California's finest basketball and football players, Kapp led his team to the Rose Bowl. He was a seventeenth-round draftee, signed with Finks' Calgary team in 1959, was traded to Vancouver two years later and played there for six seasons. In 1963 he added a Grey Cup to his credit and was named the league's Most Valuable Player. After some legal problems were ironed out (Kapp had signed a contract in 1968 to play with the Houston Oilers), the quarterback became a Viking.

Kapp joined the club just a few weeks before the start of the 1967 season, hardly enough time to get to know his teammates, much less the American pro game in general and the Vikings' style in particular. Because he didn't know Grant, Grant's coaching, his receivers, how Mick Tingelhoff centered the ball, the peculiarities of enemy defensive backs and linebackers, what kind of defense they played, etc., etc., it seemed the perfect time for caution, a chance to feel his way around some. Instead, six hours after joining the team he was telling Dale

Linebacker Jeff Siemon has a clear lane to Pittsburgh quarterback Terry Bradshaw.

The Cleveland Browns' Larry Benz wrestles with Viking veteran Bill Brown for the ball, but according to NFL rules, it aready belongs to Bill.

40

Tarkenton has just handed off to a determined Bill Brown, who is about to plunge into the Bronco defensive line.

Wally Hilgenberg has been a dependable starting linebacker for the Vikings since 1969.

Hackbart how he was going to make it big in the NFL. And he meant it, every word. This attitude is not uncommon—many newcomers to the league talk this way, but many don't make it. The difference was that Kapp wasn't a wise guy, and his words weren't just a lot of hot air.

But the newcomer had to undergo a painful familiarization process, and Viking fans' thoughts sometimes naturally turned to the slick, polished, departed Tarkenton. "I figure I can't scramble like Tarkenton, but I got to move around now and then," Kapp said, in response to comparisons. "I may not run with much speed, but I make up for it with a lot of desperation."

With lines like that, the fans soon grew to love him.

His teammates also were quickly charmed, thanks to a determined campaign on Kapp's part to win them over. He began in practice. Hackbart recalls, "Within a week of Joe's arrival, Grant was surprised to hear a general yelping and griping whenever Kapp took over at quarterback in the passing scrimmages."

"What he didn't know," Kapp explained, "was that I made some side bets with the guys that whoever intercepted a pass from me got a buck. And if I beat the defense for a touchdown, I got a buck. . . . So when I'd come in there, you'd hear the defense crowing, 'Let's get some of this guy's money,' and all kinds of noise. Well, I threw a couple for touchdowns, but the biggest noise came when Warwick intercepted one and he took off down the sidelines like Gale Sayers, so I went over to cover and I hit him a shoulder shot. I'm sure I didn't shake him up much. But in these bets for laughs, you understand, it's your personality that comes through a little. It just has to if you want to lead the team. And I wanted to lead that team, even if most of them didn't know me from Adam the first few weeks."

Though the velocity and spiral of his passes were mocked even more than Tarkenton's ever were, Kapp had a world of self-confidence. All he had to do was convince his teammates they should have the same kind of faith in him.

And convince them he did.

A Learning Year

The 1967 Vikings finished 3–8–3. It was a learning year all the way around. Kapp learned about his teammates, the league and Grant, his teammates learned about Kapp and Grant, and Grant learned about the league, his quarterback and his players. They lost games by one, four and three points, an indication of perhaps better things to come. Mistakes and penalties were reduced. A closeness and unity were forged. Something beautiful was forming.

In 1968, the Vikings finished 8–6 and won their first division championship, bowing to Baltimore, 24–14, in the playoffs. They really didn't expect to go all the way in 1968, particularly not with the powerful, once-beaten Colts as playoff opponents; but the Vikings, especially Kapp, made them work for their victory. Kapp set still-standing records for most passes attempted (44), passes completed (26) and yardage (287), hanging tough against a brutal Baltimore rush led by the menacing six-foot-seven, 295-pound Bubba Smith.

In 1969, the Vikings were 12–2 and went all the way to the Super Bowl. They were easily the NFL's finest team that year, scoring the most points in all of pro football and yielding the least. They recorded two shutouts and only once gave up more than two touchdowns, in a 24–23 season-opening upset loss to a mediocre New York Giant team. The Purple People Eaters were at their brutal, inelegant, devastating best, and so was Kapp. They staged a stirring comeback for a 23–20 victory over Los Angeles to win the league's Western Division title, then crushed Cleveland, 27–7, for their first NFL crown.

Unfortunately, Kansas City smashed the beautiful dream. The Vikings, favored by thirteen points, picked the worst time to go flat, and the Chiefs stomped them, 23–7. "We played a great team and they beat us," said Grant in his classy, no-excuse post mortem. "It's as simple as that. The reasons? They made the big plays, made no errors and moved the ball on the ground. And Len Dawson is very much underrated. He's surrounded by many stars and gets lost in the group."

A linebacker's dream: Offensive guard Ed White gets to touch the ball as he runs with a teammate's fumble.

Behind a solid wall of blockers, Fran Tarkenton (partly hidden) fades back to pass in a game against San Francisco.

Running back Clint Jones reaches back to ward off a would-be tackler.

The hard-running Ed Marinaro finds a gaping hole in the San Francisco line and powers his way up the middle.

Running back Bill Brown finds the going rough but manages to hold on to the ball.

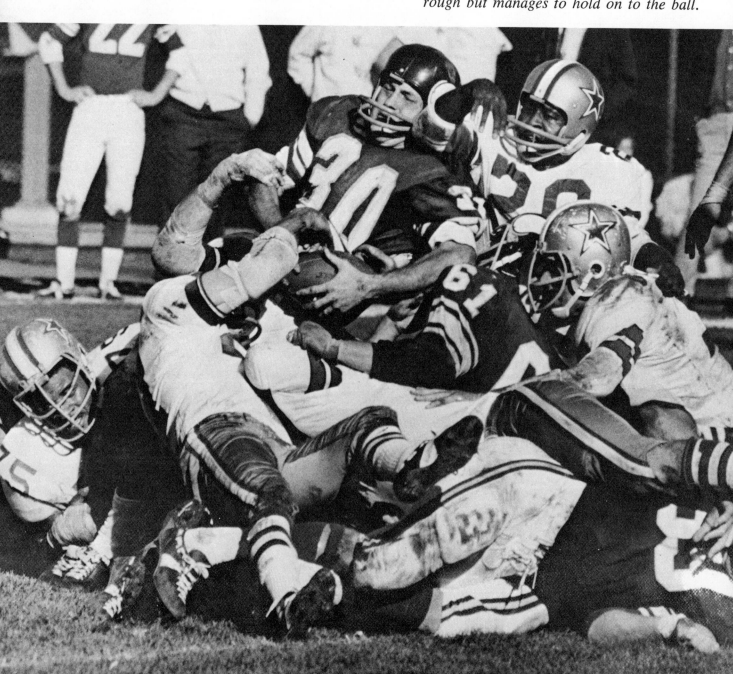

In the first game of the 1970 season, Minnesota easily beat the Chiefs, 27–10. It was, of course, eight months too late. But that year, with Gary Cuozzo at quarterback, the Vikings again finished 12–2 and had the finest record in all of pro football. They allowed just fourteen touchdowns. Even without Kapp, they were favored to win another NFL title. But this time their offense let them down against a tough, young San Francisco underdog, and they were edged, 17–14, in the first round of the playoffs.

As in the Super Bowl the year before, the Vikings again were hurt badly by mistakes. They had two passes intercepted and lost two fumbles, one late in the second quarter that allowed Bruce Gossett the chance to kick a forty-yard field goal that ultimately proved the 49er margin of victory.

An 11–3 record in 1971 ended with a 20–12 playoff loss to Dallas on Christmas Day, and the Vikings proved regular Santa Clauses to their visitors. Bob Lee had two passes intercepted, Gary Cuozzo two more, a fumble was lost, and it was all over. Dallas did not have a single turnover. The Vikings had seventeen first downs to ten for the Cowboys. They gained 311 yards to 183 by Dallas. Yet it took a fourth-quarter Viking safety and touchdown to even make the score respectable.

Grant was asked how he felt about coming so close to the top on so many occasions, yet always falling a little short. He paused, smiled and, most characteristically, rambled a bit. "We didn't play well consistently. Oh, I don't mean we played poorly. We did a lot of good things in that game, but we weren't as sharp as we could have been. . . . Look at Dallas—how many times did they get to the playoffs? Seven in a row. Six times they didn't make it. Only once did everything drop into place . . . that's the way it happens. You don't get playoff shy. You just hope you'll get back there again so you'll have another shot at it."

Running back Dave Osborn was a key factor in Minnesota's 1969 drive to the NFL championship.

the greatest .500 team

The luckless 1972 Vikings will probably be known as the greatest .500 team in history. They were preseason favorites to win the Super Bowl, as the experts reasoned that the reacquisition of Fran Tarkenton from the New York Giants would fill the one great gap in Minnesota's lineup and bring the offensive power to the level of the potent defense.

As it turned out, Tarkenton was brilliant. It was the defense that had led the NFL in the least points allowed in three consecutive years, 1969, 1970 and 1971, that let Minnesota down. In 1971, the Vikings had yielded an average of just under ten points per game during the regular season. In 1972, the number jumped to eighteen per game.

The Purple People Eaters

The heart of the Viking defense has been their front four—the Purple People Eaters, Four Norsemen, etc. From left to right, the rush line throughout Minnesota's conference reign was Carl Eller, Alan Page, Gary Larsen and Jim Marshall. Their awesome charges resulted in forty-nine quarterback sacks for 360 lost yards in 1970, twenty-eight sacks for 235 lost yards in 1971. In 1972, they upset quarterbacks only twenty-one times for ninety-two lost yards.

The loss of effectiveness by the rush line spread destructive ripples throughout the defense. The Vikings' secondary of safeties Charlie West and Paul Krause and cornerbacks Bobby Bryant and Ed Sharockman, as well as the linebacking trio of Roy Winston, Jeff Siemon and Wally Hilgenberg, are dependent for their pass coverage on a strong charge up front. If he has time, a pro quarterback is able to negate the power of a defensive unit. In the past, the Vikings' front four either tackled the passer outright or hurried him to the point of ineffectiveness. Quarterbacks used to dread a meeting with the Purple People Eaters. In 1972, however, dread turned to anticipation.

Injuries to two key players were behind the decline of the Vikings' rush. Tackle Alan Page, the first lineman ever to be named Most Valuable Player in the NFL, suffered a deep pull in the muscle of his right calf in the second pre-season game of 1971 against Buffalo. Page injured his calf again in practice early in the regular season and played the rest of the year in pain. His tremendous speed and power were seriously impaired. Continued rest was needed for the injury to heal, but the Vikings were fighting for their lives and could not afford to relinquish Page's pressure.

End Carl Eller, All-Pro for four straight seasons, hurt his right knee in training camp, which, in addition to the pain, caused a loss of his mobility. Eller reinjured the knee during a heartbreaking 16–14 loss to Miami in the third game of the season, and it was year end before he fully recovered, but by then it was too late.

Fran Tarkenton, who led the Vikings during their early years, came back in 1972 to reclaim his job as quarterback.

The Vikings' relatively short history has produced a series of quarterbacks. In this action against Green Bay, it's Gary Cuozzo's turn to be the leader.

...sive captain Jim Marshall wraps up
...n Bay ball carrier Donny Anderson,
...played for the Packers until 1972.

With two of its four members ailing, the smooth co-
ordination of the front four was disrupted. Well condi-
tioned and hard-hitting, the Viking defense usually got
tougher as a game developed and would eventually grind
an opponent into submission. Weakened as it was in
1972, the Vikings tired near the end. Minnesota lost
three games in the last quarter and pulled another out
with a desperate throw for a touchdown.

A Tough Schedule

Though the decline in defense hurt most, other factors
also conspired against the '72 Vikings. Their schedule
was probably the toughest of all the teams'. Minnesota
played against six teams that went on to win division
championships, as well as two games against Detroit, the
season's toughest runner-up.

Usually reliable field-goal kicker Fred Cox cost the
Vikings one game with a miss from twenty-six yards out
and blew three possible ties with misses of twenty-two,
thirty-two and forty-three yards. Top ball-carrier running
back Clint Jones broke a bone in his right elbow against
Chicago and missed eight remaining games.

Since the Vikings' inaugural season in 1961, Minnesota punters had kicked 681 times without having one
ball blocked. With only 2:30 gone in the first quarter of
the season's opener against the Redskins, Bill Malinchak
of Washington's punt-return team, promoted from the
taxi squad only a few days earlier, broke in and blocked
Mike Eischeid's punt, picked up the ball and raced six-
teen yards for a touchdown.

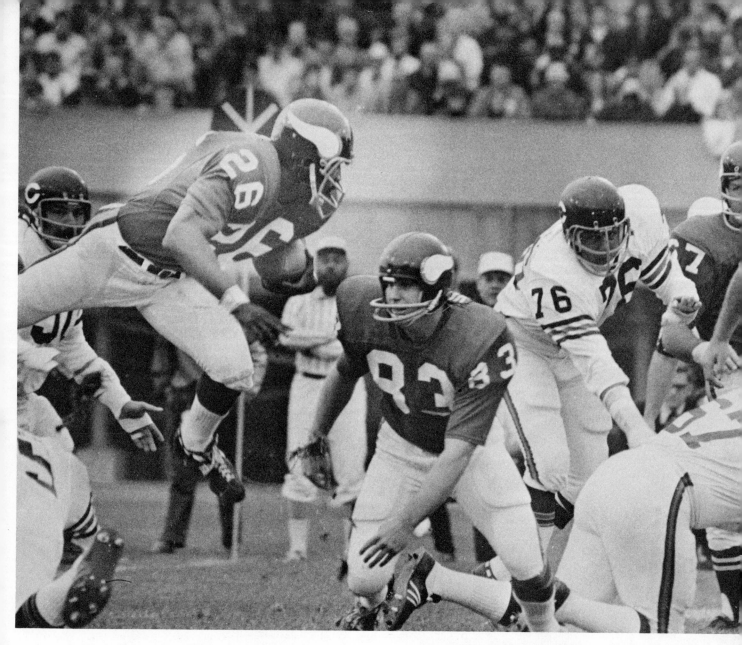

It looks like tight end Stu Voight is about to catch ball carrier Clint Jones.

With an effective rush, the Viking defense forces Dallas kicker Ron Widby to hurry his punt.

The frustrated Vikings trounced the Redskins by every statistical measure except two—mistakes made and points scored. They amassed twenty-six first downs to Washington's eleven, gained 382 total yards to 203 for Washington, ran off seventy-nine plays to the Redskins' forty-eight. Tarkenton completed eighteen of thirty-one passes for 233 yards and two touchdowns to Bill Kilmer's seven-for-seventeen, fifty-seven-yard performance. He also showed the almost 48,000 home fans he still knew how to scramble, by running three times for thirty-five yards. It was all in vain—Washington won 24–21.

Detroit, September 24, 1972

When the Vikings are hurting, the Detroit Lions make them well. The Lions tied the Vikings, 3–3, in the first quarter. The Vikings struck for two touchdowns in the second period, one on a fourteen-yard run by Dave Osborn and one on a forty-yard throw from Tarkenton to Gilliam. In the third quarter, Lion quarterback Greg Landry had three passes intercepted that led to two Viking touchdowns by Osborn and a thirty-seven-yard field goal by Cox, each errant pass evoking a chorus of boos from the sullen home crowd. It all added up to a 34–10 victory, Minnesota's ninth in a row over Detroit dating to 1967.

"One football game is certainly no indication of how good a team you are," said coach Bud Grant. Grant and everyone else would get a better indication about the Vikings after their next game with the Miami Dolphins, 1971s Super Bowl runner-up.

Bloomington, Minnesota, October 1, 1972

With just four minutes and thirty seconds to play, the Vikings held a 14–6 lead over the Dolphins. To the Vikings' fans it seemed like the good old days.

It was Bill Brown's one-yard scoring plunge early in the final period that had raised the Vikings' lead, and as the minutes ticked away, it appeared the margin would hold. But Miami quarterback Bob Griese rallied his team and drove into Minnesota territory before the Vikings were able to hold on their own forty-four-yard line.

Dolphin coach Don Shula sent Yepremian in to try a fifty-one-yard field goal. If he missed, the Dolphins were all but finished.

His line drive sailed through the uprights. It was now 14–9, with little more than four minutes to play.

Had the Vikings been able to mount a drive, they might have run out the clock. But Tarkenton, who completed only ten of twenty-three passes, was dumped five times for thirty-three yards in losses, had three of his tosses intercepted and couldn't move the Vikings forward. Minnesota had to punt.

Back came the Dolphins with a thirteen-yard run by Mercury Morris and two passes by Bob Griese to Howard Twilley, highlighting a drive that moved the ball to the Vikings' three-yard line. With 1:28 to play, Griese threw to reserve tight end Jim Mandich for the winning touchdown, Griese's sixteenth completed pass out of thirty-three thrown. The final score was 16–14.

Bloomington, Minnesota, October 8, 1972

"I get paid to make short field goals like that and not blow them," said a disconsolate Fred Cox after his twenty-six-yard attempt with two seconds to play hit the crossbar and bounced away, giving the visiting Cardinals

Green Bay wide receiver Leland Glass
doesn't have a chance at a pass reception
as Viking defensive back Charlie West is
about to effectively break up the play.

Promising guard Ed White wearily rubs his
eye during a break in a long Sunday after-
noon.

Wally Hilgenberg greets the Packers' John Brockington with open arms.

a 19–17 upset victory and dropping the record of the defending conference champion Vikings to 1–3. "I'm supposed to help us win. Sure, I can remember four or five games that I won with field goals in the final seconds. But that is irrelevant. Those are gone. The only thing that counts is I missed the field goal that could have won the St. Louis game for us."

Galling as the loss was to Cox, he need not have taken the full responsibility. In years past, the Vikings could have counted on their defense to hold the Cardinals and preserve the lead, but, as noted, the Vikings' defense was not the rock it had once been.

Denver, October 15, 1972

The law of averages finally began to work for the Vikings. Fran Tarkenton hit Gene Washington with a thirty-one-yard touchdown pass with just seventeen seconds remaining in the game, to give Minnesota a 23–20 victory and keep the struggling winners' playoff hopes barely alive.

Chicago, October 23, 1972

The Vikings broke on top in the opening period when Tarkenton connected with Gilliam on a forty-four-yard scoring pass. But the Bears roared back in the second quarter on Mac Percival's twenty-one-yard field goal and quarterback Bobby Douglass' four-yard touchdown pass to sophomore running back Jim Harrison to take a 10–7 halftime lead.

The best the Vikings could do in the second half was to even the score at ten on a twenty-one-yard field goal by Cox in the third quarter.

In the fourth quarter, Mac Percival kicked a twenty-yard field goal, and the Bears led 13–10. Tarkenton threw what looked like a five-yard touchdown pass to tight end John Beasley. As is common in such situations, everyone looked around for a flag before reacting. Seeing none, the Vikings began a wild victory dance on the sidelines and the field.

At the same time, Chicago tackle Andy Rice was screaming at the ref and pointing downfield. Out came a yellow flag. Rice had told the official that Viking guard Ed White had been downfield illegally, the ref agreed and the play was called back. With seven seconds to play, Cox blew a twenty-seven-yard field goal and the Vikings were losers, 13–10.

Green Bay, October 29, 1972

Reversing their habit of blowing leads, the Vikings rallied from a 10–0 first-quarter deficit, and then again facing a 13–10 score in the fourth quarter, to achieve a decisive 27–13 victory over the Packers. Matched with Detroit's loss to Dallas, it put Minnesota just a game behind the Conference's co-leaders, Detroit and Green Bay, at midseason. Most encouraging of all, it was the Viking defense that was largely responsible for the victory over Green Bay.

Bloomington, November 5, 1972

After watching three straight losses, Viking home fans had something to cheer about as they watched their team roll up a 20–0 halftime lead and go on to an easy 37–6 victory over the New Orleans Saints. For the hard-pressed Vikings themselves, it was their first truly easy game since the 34–10 win over Detroit in September, and it kept them just a game behind the Lions and Packers in the increasingly tense division race.

Minnesota was a standout at offense and defense. Tarkenton had one of his finest days, completing nineteen passes out of twenty-six throws for 178 yards and two touchdowns. The Vikings ran off forty-two plays in the first half to twenty-two by New Orleans, a graphic indication of how thoroughly they dominated the contest.

In a clash of immovable forces, Jim Marshall goes against the Cowboys' Lee Roy Caffey on a kickoff return.

60

Wally Hilgenberg and Karl Kassulke make a valiant effort to block Patriot Charlie Gogolak's placekick.

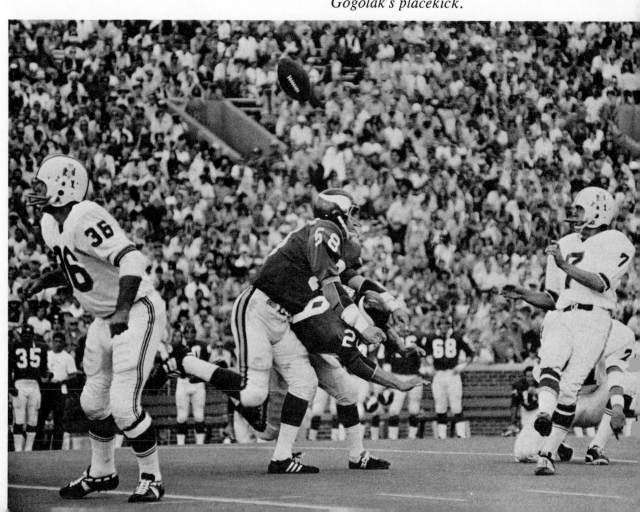

Exciting prospect Ed Marinaro takes a handoff from Fran Tarkenton and runs behind the blocking of backfield mate Oscar Reed.

Mick Tingelhoff, signed as a free agent, has become a Minnesota Vikings institution.

Bloomington, November 12, 1972

The Vikings met Detroit for the second time in the season and made it their tenth straight win over the Lions.

"All we had to do was kick a field goal to win the game," whispered Detroit coach Joe Schmidt, who still looked in shock a half hour after entering the tomblike visitors' dressing area. "We should be able to kick a field goal. At least we should get the ball in the air and have a chance."

Later, after viewing films of the play, Schmidt would conclude that it was a high snap from center Ed Flanagan that gave Bryant time for "another step and a half." Bryant, however, thought the key to the play was the way linebacker Wally Hilgenberg took out the Lions' blocking back. "I came in from the extreme outside. No one touched me on the play. That gave me a straight shot at the ball."

No one was more surprised—or disgusted—by Bryant's game-saver than Errol Mann, who could have shared a few beers and tears with Cox. "I've never been so sure of anything in my life," said Mann, a six-year veteran. "I knew when I kicked it that it was no more than two feet off dead center. Greg [Landry] handled the snap right, the laces were in the right direction and I was just about on time."

He never saw Bryant coming. "My job is to look at the ball," he said. "I didn't know anything was wrong until I heard a slap on the ball."

Early in the game it appeared the Vikings were headed for a painful defeat. They had a 10–0 lead in the third quarter. Then Oscar Reed fumbled on the Lions' four-yard line, the usually reliable Gene Washington dropped what appeared to be certain touchdown passes and two additional fumbles by rookie Ed Marinaro pushed the Vikings against the wall. Lion quarterback Landry hit Larry Walton with quick scoring passes of forty-eight and twenty yards midway through the third period, and the Lions led 14–10.

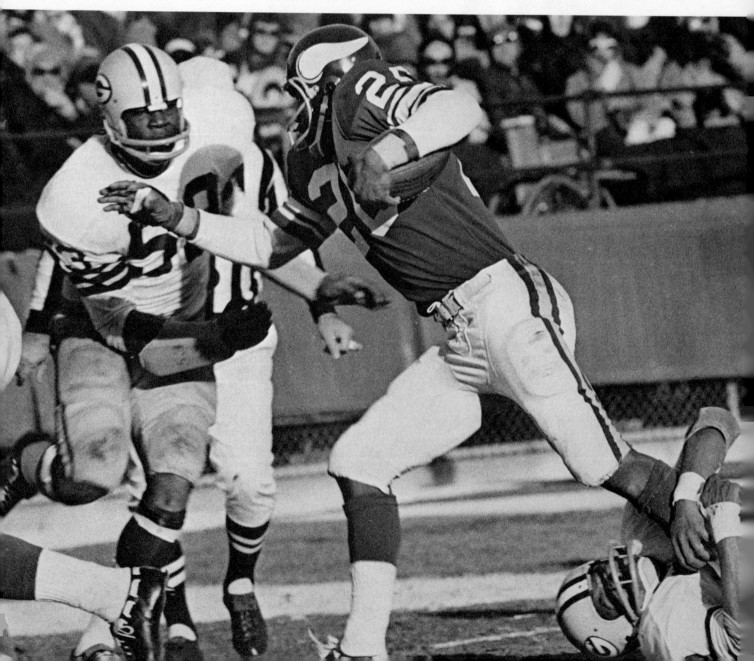

Carl Kassulke makes a low tackle on a Green Bay ball carrier.

Cox brought in three points early in the final quarter with an eighteen-yard field goal, and then it was the Vikings' turn to capitalize on a fumble by the Lions' great tight end Charlie Sanders. Minnesota linebacker Roy Winston recovered it, and Cox thrilled the crowd with a twenty-three-yard field goal that gave the Vikings the lead again, and the game.

Los Angeles, November 19, 1972

In this meeting of two of pro football's traditional defensive giants, the Vikings edged the Rams, 45–41.

"It wasn't exactly the kind of contest you'd expect from a couple of teams ranked number one and number two defensively," Bud Grant said. "Why the scoring? The weather, I guess. We took our July offense out of mothballs. Usually, at this time of year, we're in our cold weather offense, playing in the snow."

The Rams concentrated on stopping Minnesota's ground game, so Tarkenton passed . . . and passed . . . and passed. He completed fourteen of his twenty-eight throws for 319 yards, including three long second-half touchdown passes of seventy-six yards to Bill Brown, seventy yards to wide receiver John Henderson and sixty-six yards to Gilliam, which put Minnesota ahead, 45–34, midway through the final quarter.

The Packers and Lions also won their games, so the tight three-way race for the division's playoff spot remained unchanged with four games to play. A 1972 NFL innovation was the introduction of the wildcard entry to the playoffs, by which the runner-up with the best record in the NFC and in the AFC would join the six division champions in the playoffs. With four losses behind them, the Vikings could hardly count on that. They would have to win the race outright. With three of the four remaining games against teams leading, or tied for the lead of their respective divisions, and the other game against the dangerously unpredictable Chicago Bears, Minnesota faced a most imposing challenge.

The tough, rapidly maturing AFC Central Division leaders, the Pittsburgh Steelers, were on the verge of winning their first title of any kind in forty years of pro

Clint Jones has the ball and is determined to gain more yardage in spite of strong Green Bay efforts to the contrary.

football play. With their great physical exuberance, strong defense and young players, the Steelers resembled the Packers in many ways.

Pittsburgh, November 26, 1972

The Vikings lost 23–10 to the Steelers. After 331 consecutive successful holds over eight-plus seasons, Paul Krause bobbled not one but two snaps on abortive five- and seven-yard field goal attempts.

The game was filled with all sorts of other untoward events. Two Viking defenders ran into each other and spoiled what should have been a sure interception. Two other Vikings did the same and enabled Steeler Rookie of the Year Franco Harris to run sixty-one yards in the fourth quarter to set up the touchdown that broke a 10–10 tie. The best thing in the game for Minnesota was Tarkenton's twenty-four successful passes out of forty-three throws for 235 yards. That, and the fact that the Packers lost to the Redskins and stayed only one game ahead of the Vikings.

Bloomington, December 3, 1972

It's hard to say what chilled the Bears more, the minus-two-degree temperature or Minnesota's defense. In a heartening display of their old-time expertise, the Vikings limited Chicago to five first downs, one net yard passing on two completions in thirteen attempts by Bobby Douglass and only ninety yards on the ground. In contrast, Tarkenton frolicked in the snow, connecting on twenty-one of his thirty-nine passes for 261 yards and a touchdown. It added up to a 23–10 Viking victory, leading to a dramatic confrontation for first place with the Packers.

Bloomington, December 10, 1972

One look at Alan Page in the game's closing minutes told the story. Dirty, bloody and sweaty, the giant tackle sat on the bench cradling his head in his huge hands, not even looking up at the field. Page had been ejected by the officials after arguing violently that he had been

Constantly manning the earphones, coach Bud Grant incorporates the advice of his assistants in planning the strategy for each game.

Clint Jones has a jarring collision with an unidentified Packer defender.

Tight end Stu Voight sprints all alone past the flag for a Viking touchdown.

The action gets a bit frantic on a kickoff against the Packers. Among others in precarious positions, Ed Marinaro (49) has been upended.

drawn offsides by Packer center Cal Withrow's habit of picking the ball up before snapping on punts. Without doubt, Page believed he was right.

The game, sheer frustration, was played in Packer-Viking weather. The temperature was zero, but a nine-mile-per-hour wind created a wind-chill factor that made it feel eighteen below and brought out the colorful ski masks, hoods, parkas and other protective gear of Minnesota Decembers.

After a scoreless first quarter, the Vikings drew first blood when tight end Stu Voight took a handoff from Tarkenton on an end-around and outraced Packer defensive end Alden Roche to the corner flag for a touchdown.

The score was still 7–0 as the first half began to draw to a close, and Viking hopes began to soar. The defense was holding. Perhaps happy days were here again.

Then Green Bay came to life. The Packers drove from their own twenty-eight-yard line to Minnesota's three as the second quarter's final seconds ticked away, only to be set back by a most inopportune fifteen-yard penalty. Krause intercepted Scott Hunter's pass on his own three-yard line on the last play of the half, touching off hysteria in the stands. Down on the field, however, no Viking celebrated and no Packer hung his head. In the mysterious ebbs and flows of a football game, the tide had turned in Green Bay's favor, and somehow both clubs sensed it. The Packers, whose main offensive flaw was the lack of a reliable passing game, had showed they had the guys and the strength to move the Vikings on the ground. "That drive gave us a whole new incentive," said Packer linebacker Dave Robinson, one of the few veterans left from the vintage Vince Lombardi teams.

Packer rookie Chester Marcol, who kicked a league-record thirty-three field goals in his first year and proved a big 1972 asset to Green Bay, booted a thirty-six yarder to cut the Viking lead to 7–3.

The gritty Tarkenton tried to rally his mates. He threw and hit Bill Brown on the Minnesota forty-six. But Packer linebacker Fred Carr also hit Brown, jarred the ball loose, picked it up and ran to the Vikings' twenty-eight. Six plays later, Green Bay quarterback Scott

Hunter put his helmet on guard Mal Snider's rump and followed him one yard into the end zone for a 10–7 Packer lead.

Again Tarkenton tried to reverse the game's ominous trend with his arm, but this time he went to the well once too often. Rookie Packer cornerback Willie Buchanon picked off a pass intended for Gilliam, one of three Green Bay interceptions to go with three sackings of the over-worked Tarkenton, and returned it from the Viking forty-nine to the twenty-four. A pass interference call against Minnesota brought it to the nine—and three plays later Lane went over untouched from the three for the touchdown that crowned a new champion. Marcol booted two field goals of forty-two yards and ten yards to give the game to the Packers, 23–10. The Packers and Vikings had stood eyeball to eyeball and it was the Vikings who blinked.

San Francisco, December 17, 1972

The season ended with a 20–17 loss to the 49ers.

The Vikings led, 17–6, going into the fourth quarter on Tarkenton's eighteen-yard touchdown pass to Ed Marinaro, his thirty-one yarder to Gilliam and a forty-three-yard field goal by Cox.

Fighting for the NFC Western Division title, the 49ers replaced Steve Spurrier at quarterback with John Brodie, who was making his first appearance after a lengthy recovery from an ankle injury. Brodie hit Gene Washington (no relation to the Viking of the same name) with a twenty-four-yard touchdown pass, then, with twenty-five seconds to play, threw a two-yarder to Dick Wichter for the winning score.

Hope For The Future

A year that began with high hopes ended in frustration and a heartbreaking defeat. Viewed another way, the frustration and heartbreak could lead to the kind of self-examination and analysis that brings new strength and a concerted effort to correct deficiencies and weaknesses. No one blew the Vikings off the field in 1972.

70

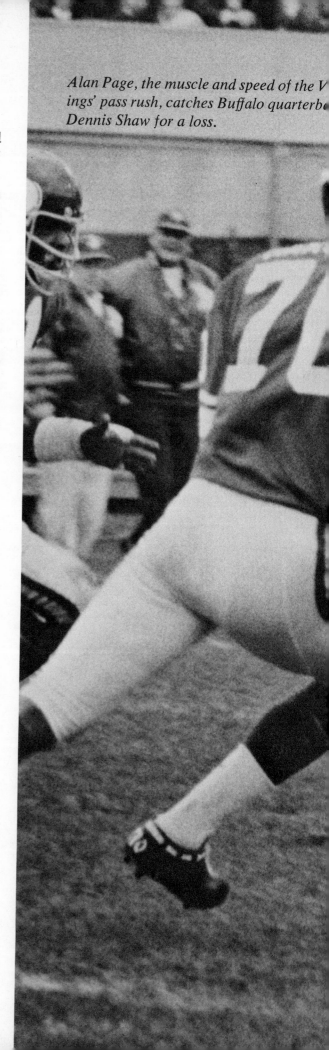

Alan Page, the muscle and speed of the Vikings' pass rush, catches Buffalo quarterback Dennis Shaw for a loss.

Oscar Reed, leading ground-gainer for
Vikings in 1972, eludes the tackle of Gr
Bay's Bob Brown.

Guard Milt Sunde (64) clears the way for
running back Clint Jones.

Bill Brown is one of the toughest and most determined runners in the NFL, and he can be depended upon to pick up that key third-down yardage.

Cornerback Bobby Bryant steals a pass from Dave Hampton, then of Green Bay

. . . And scampers down the sidelines.

Bob Lee has been a capable backup quarterback for the Vikings over the years.

Dave Osborn cuts to open field around two pursuing Cleveland Browns.

Safety Karl Kassulke (29) intercepts a pass with a little help from linebacker Roy Winston.

Cornerback Bob Bryant appears a little miffed with himself even though Green Bay's Jon Staggers didn't reach the pass either.

Dave Osborn has been a steady and consistent fixture in the Viking backfield for many years.

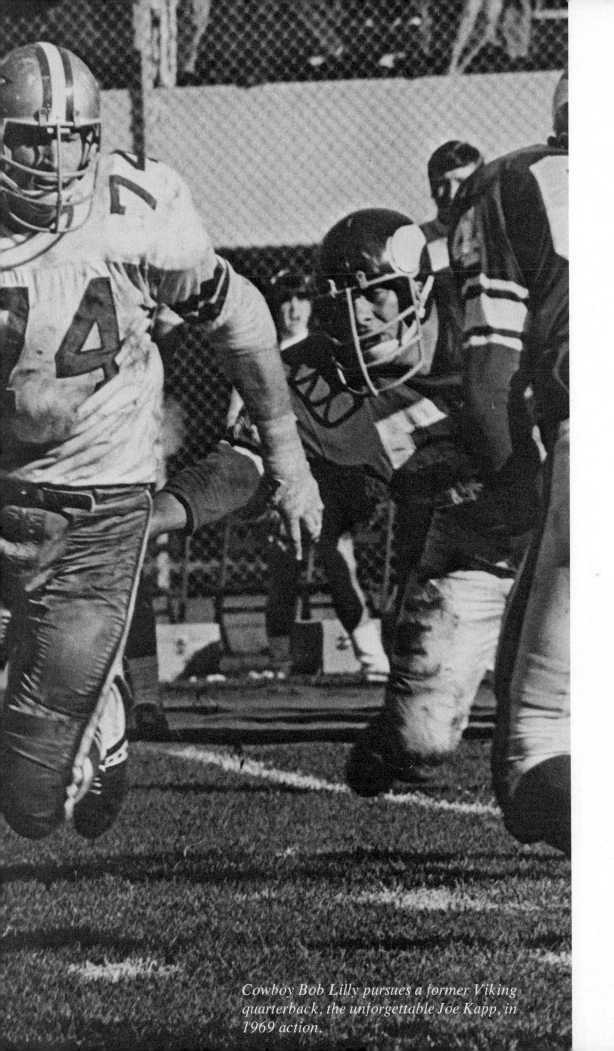

Cowboy Bob Lilly pursues a former Viking quarterback, the unforgettable Joe Kapp, in 1969 action.

Fran Tarkenton follows through on a pass as Ron Yary (73) and Grady Alderman (67) keep out two Packers.

Tarkenton, offensive captain of the Vikings, gets a clarification on the referee's call.

ng into the 1973 season, Fran Tarken-
had thrown for more than 30,000
ds and had a completion record of
er than 55 percent.

Dave Osborn, carrying the ball in one huge hand, deftly avoids the tackle of Miami linebacker Mike Kolen.

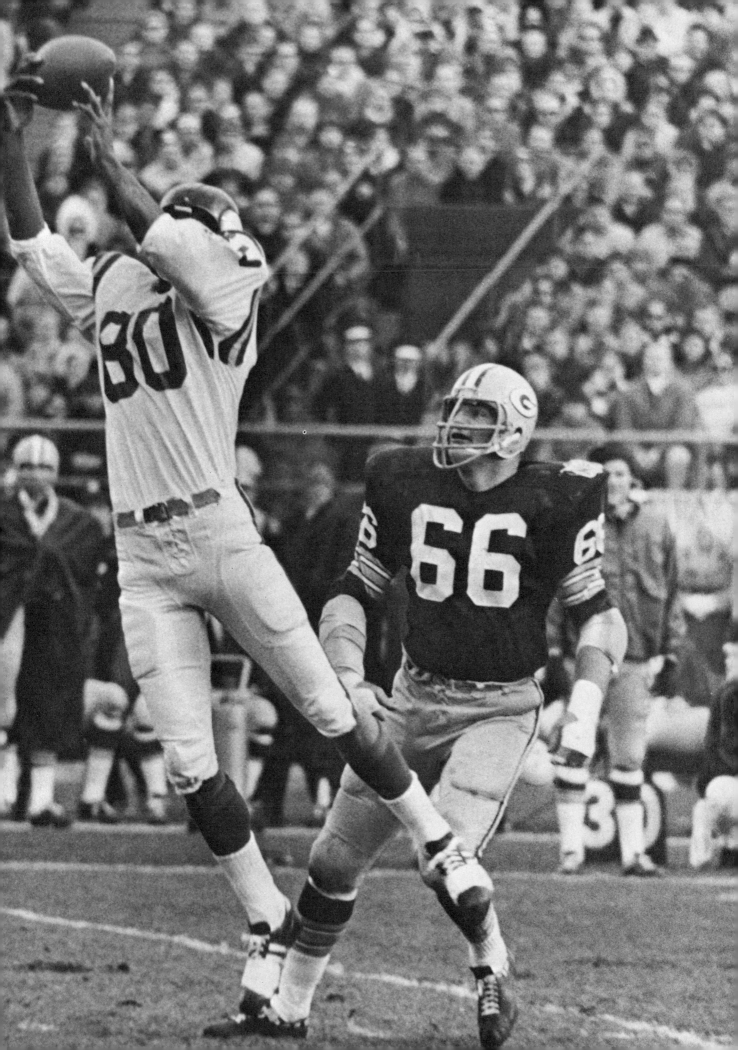

*As of 1972, Bill Brown was the leading
active rusher in the NFC.*

Jim Marshall (70) and Wally Hilgenberg (58) wrestle with the Rams' Roman Gabriel in a 1969 playoff action.

Clint Jones: "I love running with the ball."

The Minnesota Vikings' Purple People Eaters.

Defensive back Charlie West takes a well-deserved breather.

the valiant vikings

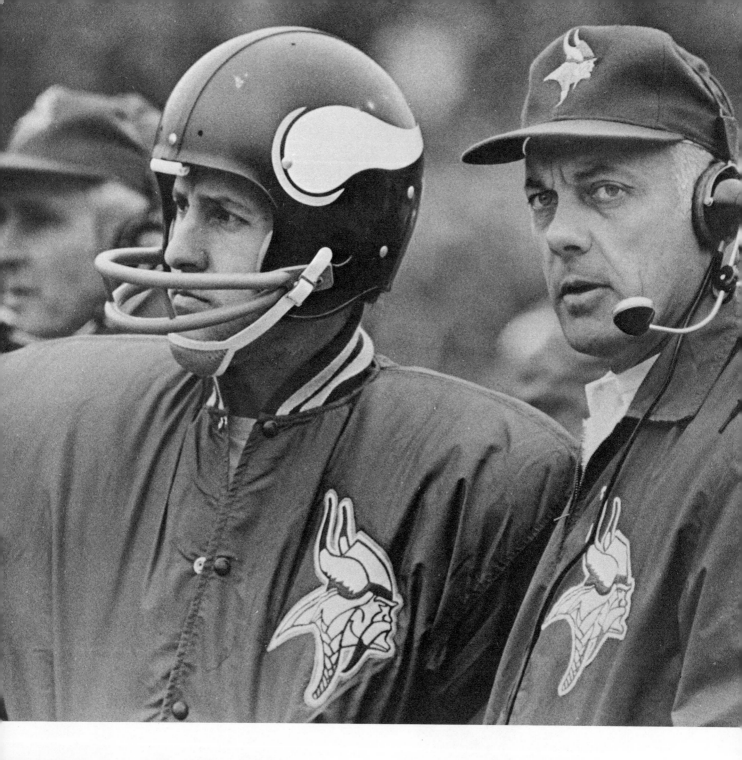

Tarkenton and two members of his offensive line, tackle Grady Alderman (67) and guard Ed White, go over last-minute game-plan preparations.

ternfaced coach Bud Grant and his quar-
erback Fran Tarkenton. Are they think-
g about a championship for Minnesota?

fran tarkenton

Fran Tarkenton calls signals in his first stint as a Viking.

"Coming back to the Vikings is like slipping into an old shoe," said quarterback Fran Tarkenton in 1972 after five years of playing for the New York Giants.

Tarkenton brought an offensive punch to the Vikings which had an almost unbeatable defense. That the 1972 season ended with a 7–7 record cannot be attributed to his lack of superior playing ability. He completed 58 percent of his 371 passes for a total gain of 2,651 yards and eighteen touchdowns which solidified his standing through 1972 as the fifth leading passer in football history. To everyone's surprise it was Minnesota's defense that weakened that year.

In Fran's first hitch with the Vikings, from 1961 through 1966, his method of play added the word "scramble" to pro football's vocabulary. With a weak offensive line, Fran was really running for his life in the beginning. Tarkenton had fine individual seasons, but not once did the team finish as high as .500.

Coach Van Brocklin and Tarkenton didn't see eye to eye too often and in 1967 Fran was traded to the Giants. He had five personally excellent seasons in New York although the Giants were going through a difficult period. He yearned to play with a team that had a better shot at the Super Bowl.

While Tarkenton has always been selected for the Pro Bowl, only two of his eleven seasons prior to 1972 had he played for a team with a defense that yielded fewer than 300 points. In the three seasons before Tarkenton rejoined the Vikings, they hadn't given up over 150 points. They gave up 139 in 1971, and a league record low of 133 in 1969. Unfortunately, they scored only 245 points that year, ranking eighteenth in the league. An injury to the Vikings' best runner, Clint Jones, left Fran virtually without a ground game, but he did manage to put 301 points on the board for Minnesota. In pro football history the only man to average six yards or more per rush for more than 500 carries is—Francis A. Tarkenton.

While his passes are not always perfect spirals thrown with a bulletlike velocity, through 1972 he'd thrown them for more than 30,000 yards and had a career completion mark of 55 percent. This is much better than almost all the quarterbacks who throw beautiful picture passes. To amass these impressive running and passing figures, Tarkenton has had to be more than just durable.

Lionel Aldridge of Green Bay tries in vain to bring down the Original Scrambler, Fran Tarkenton.

Tarkenton drives opposing linemen crazy with his scrambling style.

alan page

Page is so quick he is extremely adept at tackling fast runners in the open field. Here he nabs Larry Schreiber of San Francisco.

Alan Page played both offense and defense in high school in Canton, Ohio, and was All-American at Notre Dame. But when he was asked if he'd like a shot at playing offense in the NFL, the Vikings' outstanding defensive tackle vehemently said, "Zero! There is no way you could get me to play offense. It doesn't have the same quality, the same reckless abandon."

Reckless abandon. That is the best way to describe the way the six-foot-four, 245-pound Page plays football. Perhaps the quickest off the ball among the big men in the NFL, he explodes on the snap and has often run by —or over—the unfortunate player assigned to block him, so quickly that his opponent doesn't have a chance

Defensive tackle Alan Page was the National Football League's MVP in 1971.

...fensive tackle Alan Page is one of the ...instays of the Minnesota defense and a ...ember of one of the toughest front fours ... pro football.

to come out of his starting stance. He has been described by some knowing coaches as "perhaps the best player in pro football."

To recognize football's infantry, the Associated Press decided in 1971 to name a Most Valuable Defensive Player as well as the MVP award, which usually went to a runner, quarterback or receiver. As it turned out, the AP could have waited another year to reward the unpublicized foot soldiers of the defense. For in 1971, Alan Page won both of the wire service's awards.

Page was surprised to learn that this unprecedented honor had been bestowed upon him, but he was about the only one.

"Alan is a truly remarkable athlete," says Viking coach Bud Grant, who chose Page as Minnesota's number one draft choice in 1967, and made him the only rookie starter he'd ever had to that time. "He is able to do things you wouldn't expect of him. He has that capacity to rise up and make the big play when you need it most."

Page has shown spectacular progress with each passing year. From a 270-pound rookie, he turned into a lean and mean 245-pound sophomore star on defense, one of football's greatest. In 1969, he was an All-NFC selection, was All-Pro the next season, and just about won everything in sight in 1971. Throughout the 1972 season he was handicapped by a pulled calf muscle, an injury that requires rest, yet isn't destructive enough to keep a man out of the lineup. Even so, he still earned All-Conference honors. Once asked the profession he would enjoy next to football, Page replied, "Drag racing! I'm wild about cars!"

More reckless abandon.

107

jim marshall

The Vikings' famed defense buries t. opposition.

Jim Marshall forces former great Bart Sta of Green Bay to his knees.

Jim Marshall's goal is simple: It's the quarterback. "He's the enemy," says the six-foot-four, 252-pound Viking defensive end, "and we're out to destroy him!"

Marshall has been in the demolition business a long time. One of the Vikings' earliest and best trades was made for him and five other players from Cleveland for several draft choices in 1961, Minnesota's inaugural season. An All-American at Ohio State in 1958, Marshall had played a year of pro ball in Canada before signing as the Browns' fourth-round pick in the 1960 draft. He played in every Cleveland game, and in eleven years has never missed a Viking game. It seems fair to conclude that Marshall the Destroyer is virtually indestructible himself.

"Nobody in football is faster coming off that defensive line than Jim Marshall," Norm Van Brocklin said in 1962. "The man is sudden, that's about all you can call him." Jim Parker, the great former Baltimore Colt of-

Another member of the Purple People Eaters is defensive end Jim Marshall. Through the 1972 season, he had never missed a Viking game.

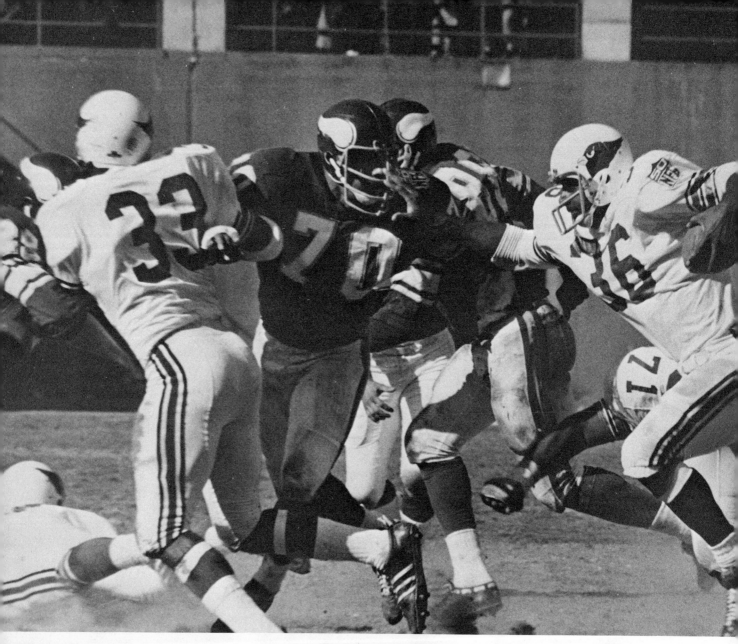

Though Marshall has suffered much pain in his time, nothing seems to keep him down or out of a game.

*m Marshall (70) easily brushes off a
'ocker and runs straight into MacArthur
ane (36), now of Green Bay, who played
r St. Louis in 1969.*

fensive lineman, and now a Hall-of-Famer, sadly agreed with Van Brocklin's assessment. "I couldn't keep him out of our backfield," Parker said after Marshall turned him every way but inside out in a 1962 game. "I asked him if he would just slow down a little."

Marshall didn't slow down then and still hasn't. The captain of Minnesota's defense, he is called "one of *the* great football players" by coach Bud Grant, who wastes no words. Like Carl Eller, who mans the other Viking defensive end post, Marshall's greatest assets are his extreme quickness and his determination not to be beaten by anyone. Once, as a youngster in Columbus, Ohio, he ran away from a fight. His father told him, "I don't care whether you get whipped or not, you go back there and fight." Marshall went back, fought, won and hasn't conceded defeat since.

He has needed every bit of his considerable pluck and self-confidence to survive near death from a bout of encephalitis, an accidentally self-inflicted bullet wound in his stomach in January, 1964, an automobile accident in which the driver of the other car was killed, severe financial reverses in the early 1960's, a grape that lodged in his throat and necessitated hospitalization, and a snowmobile accident in the Rockies, followed by a blizzard that stranded Marshall and fifteen others for twenty-four hours and cost one man his life. Oh, yes, a sixty-six-yard run the wrong way with a fumble that cost the Vikings a safety.

It almost seems as though Marshall has a death wish, but he actually enjoys life to the fullest. His interests are as varied as his talents. He paints, sculpts, writes poetry, plays chess, dabbles in karate and judo, studies Zen Buddhism and flies an airplane. He has sold wigs and mobile telephones and once tried to buy a used German U-boat. But his favorite activity, next to destroying quarterbacks, is skydiving.

"The first time I jumped was the first time I felt completely free in the deepest sense," he says. "Within."

Considering his past effectiveness, the Vikings should give thanks the chute opened.

Norm Van Brocklin once said, "Nobody in football is faster coming off that line than Jim Marshall."

Gary Larsen is noted for his ability to wait back and discourage the draw play.

gary larsen

Before a game, defensive tackle Gary Larsen traditionally sits on the bench and talks to himself. The more he talks, the angrier he becomes.

On every front four there is one tackle who "stays home"—that is, delays his charge just long enough to discourage the draw, the screen or the quick trap, all traditional offensive weapons designed to burn an over zealous pass rush. On the Vikings, six-foot-five, 260 pound Gary Larsen stays home. Feel sorry for any back he catches breaking and entering.

Larsen, obtained from Los Angeles in 1965, entered pro ball in 1963. He is the strongest of the four behemoths who comprise the rush line. He is also the most hostile at the start of a game. He sits and talks to himself before the opening kickoff, and the more he talks the more hostile he gets.

Gary Larsen (77) and Alan Page (88) force Bob Griese of Miami into a difficult position.

"I always say to myself, 'This is my livelihood. That guard in front of me is going to take the bread out of my kids' mouths if he beats me,'" Larsen explains. "I hate to say I hate anybody, but he's standing in the way of a championship, and I don't like that.

"Friends ask, 'What does it feel like before a game?' I can't describe it. I am nervous, I can't eat. You know how a wolf paces in a zoo? That's how I feel. I am caged in the dressing room. I want to get started. It's violent. It's the closest thing to war we have. I am going out there in combat. Then I get that first hit, and it's over, and I feel great."

Larsen was born in Fargo, North Dakota, was raised in Moorhead, Minnesota, and attended Concordia College in St. Paul for a year before joining the Marines. "Call it corny, but I loved the dress blues," he says. "I also wanted to see if I could take it. It was harder than I thought, but it helped me a lot more than it hurt. Pro football is not much different physically from college ball. The mental part, that is what is tough. Forty men can make the team, and sixty-five to seventy try out. Always, one guy ready to take your job. You may have all the talent, but you have to be mentally tough. You have to shrug off a lot of stuff. Some rookies can't. They sneak out of the dorms in the middle of the night. The Marines helped my mental toughness."

Add that tough-mindedness to a massive body and a self-induced fury and you have a first-rate defensive tackle.

carl eller

The nickname "Moose" suggests a ponderous, hulking individual, so it really doesn't fit Carl Eller. He is swift, graceful and powerful. He is also considered the barometer of the Vikings' defense. When he performs well, so does the rest of the line.

A swollen right knee kept the six-foot-six, 250-pound Eller from being as disruptive to opposing teams in 1972 as he had been in some of his eight other pro seasons. As a result, the entire Viking defense suffered. Still, Eller's play was good enough to make him All-Pro and be selected for the Pro Bowl for the fifth straight year. In his early thirties, Eller has a magnificent physique which, combined with his fierce determination to excel, promises several more years of top caliber play.

Carl Eller and Gary Larsen combine to bring down Bart Starr.

Carl Eller says, "What I've got to do is break through, whatever protection they try to put up against me. I've got to be able to get past them. I've got to become unstoppable."

Carl Eller has been an All-Pro defensive end for many years.

It has been said of Carl Eller, the Vikings' great defensive end, that "he is the barometer of the Minnesota defense."

Eller was the Vikings' number-one draft choice out of the University of Minnesota in 1964. A 265-pound All-America who could run the 40-yard dash in an unbelievable 4.5 seconds, his clocking is exceeded only by the fastest pro backs. Coach Norm Van Brocklin initially said that Eller's great natural talent should earn him All-Pro status, but the Dutchman's words of praise turned critical when he detected what he considered a lack of aggression in his powerful young prodigy. Eller, disagreeing, said, "It takes a couple of years for a defensive lineman to mature, to adjust." Judging by his subsequent development, he was right.

Eller's ultimate goal as a football player? "I've got to break through or break down whatever protection is put up against me—two or even three men, whatever," he once said. "I've got to be able to get past them. I've got to become . . . *unstoppable.*"

According to Viking teammate Ron Yary, an All-Pro offensive tackle, Eller is not far from achieving his ambition. "I have more problems in practice with Eller than against any defensive end I've ever faced in a game," says Yary, who goes head-to-head with Eller in practice. "Carl has speed, quickness, agility, size and strength. The only place you can take on Eller is between his chest and his abdomen. Try to hit him higher and he has the strength to grab your shoulders and throw you off balance. All he needs is a split second and he is past you. You can't cut him (throw a block at his legs) because he has the quickness to dodge or step over the block. That leaves you lying there feeling foolish while he's taking a shot at the quarterback. You know, he's going to make me a good tackle."

ron yary

Just as Ron Yary has good things to say about Carl Eller, Eller has the same for Yary. Eller returns Yary's compliment: "Because he is tall, six-foot-five, you can't reach over him or around him. He has good balance and the ability to recover quickly. That makes it hard for a defensive end. He makes his move and recovers quickly enough so that he doesn't lose control. Ron has strength so you can't run over him. It is suicide to charge straight at him. Maybe his strongest point is blocking on the run, straight ahead. That's when he uses his strength to best advantage."

Viking general manager Jim Finks and coach Bud Grant sum up their feelings about the All-Pro tackle in their usually succinct fashion. Says Finks, "I wouldn't trade Yary for any tackle in the league." Says Grant, "Yary is the best tackle in football."

That's what the Vikings envisioned Yary becoming when they selected him first in the 1968 draft. His college credentials were impeccable: two-time All-American at the University of Southern California and winner of the Outland Trophy as the nation's top college lineman, Yary was a blue-chip prospect in the eyes of knowing pro scouts.

"To appreciate Yary, you have to watch the films," says a Viking teammate. "He's amazing. He destroys people. I've seen plays where he cleans out the defensive end and takes the linebackers with him."

In response Yary is properly modest about such a bouquet. "There are a lot of good offensive linemen in the league," he says. "It's a matter of blocking on every play. I don't believe there is anyone that much better than anyone else. There are too many good ones around the league."

Yary, however, does sometimes reveal the kind of confidence found in truly great players. Viking offensive line coach John Michels remembers a telling remark by Yary during a 1971 game.

"We were talking about what we were going to do on the next series, and Ron said, 'You tell me where you want me to move my guy and I'll move him . . . sideways, forward or backward.' "

Tackle Ron Yary (73) can't do much about blocking for teammate Dave Osborn.

paul krause

In his first nine NFL seasons, free safety Paul Krause made fifty-eight interceptions, heading him toward all-time pro football leader Em Tunnell's seventy-nine. A Krause interception has its own trademark. After almost every such catch, the disappointed quarterback trudges sadly toward the bench, spreads his hands in a gesture of blamelessness and moans to the coach, "I didn't see him."

It's no accident. Krause plans it that way.

"We try to disguise our defense so that the quarterback doesn't know what we are going to do until the ball is snapped and we move into it," he explains. "I try to be someplace where he doesn't expect to find the free safety. Position is important. I know how much ground I can cover, and I know how fast I can go. I might try to lure a passer into throwing to my area by laying off a guy, as long as I know I can get to the spot and make the play. When the other team doesn't go long, you find yourself moving up a little, trying to cheat. That can be dangerous, but again it's a matter of knowing how far you can challenge the passer and still be able to recover to make the play without getting burned. You can't make your move for an interception until the ball is thrown— although you can favor one side or the other. If the quarterback pumps his arm and doesn't throw, and you have committed yourself to a short pass, the receiver goes long and it's a touchdown. The most important thing for a free safety to remember is that his teammates —the cornerbacks and strong safety—are depending on him being back there should they run into trouble or release a receiver who goes beyond their zone of coverage."

Known as the Cool Hand Luke of the Viking defense, the six-foot-three, 210-pound Krause was a Washington Redskin second-round draft choice from Iowa in 1964. As a rookie he was All-Pro and led the NFL with his twelve interceptions. He played for the Redskins until 1968, when the Vikings obtained him for tight end Marlin McKeever. He has played in five Pro Bowl games.

Krause might have found himself in the World Series. He explains, "I was always a baseball player first, a center-fielder, and I wanted to play in the big leagues." He says, "I could hit—.418 one year. I was a switch-hitter, so the curve didn't bother me. But I was playing football, too, and one day I ruined my shoulder—tore everything in it. After that, it had to be football."

Actually, he compromised. Krause now plays center-field for the Minnesota Vikings.

Carl Eller runs in to assist teammates Roy Winston (60) and Paul Krause (22) in bringing down the ball carrier.

gene washington

Gene Washington was once a high scho[ol] basketball player who, at only six-foo[t] two, could dunk the ball. His jumping ab[il]ity has helped him immeasurably as [a] football receiver.

At one time there were two segregated high schools in Baytown, Texas—George Washington Carver for the blacks and, across the street, Robert E. Lee for the whites. "We used the same stadium for football, track and baseball," Washington recalls. "We even had the same dressing rooms, but we trained at different times and they played on Saturdays, while we played on Fridays."

Washington won *black* all-state honors in basketball, football and baseball and was the *black* state hurdles champion. His football team won three *black* conference championships and one *black* state title. "I've got to be careful how I say this," Washington says, "because it's ticklish. I don't want it to sound like I had this overpowering need to prove I was better than white kids. I didn't. But I had succeeded only against a certain percentage of all the athletes in Texas, the black ones. I had to wonder about myself. Would I still be a champion if I had to compete against all the athletes in Texas—black and white?"

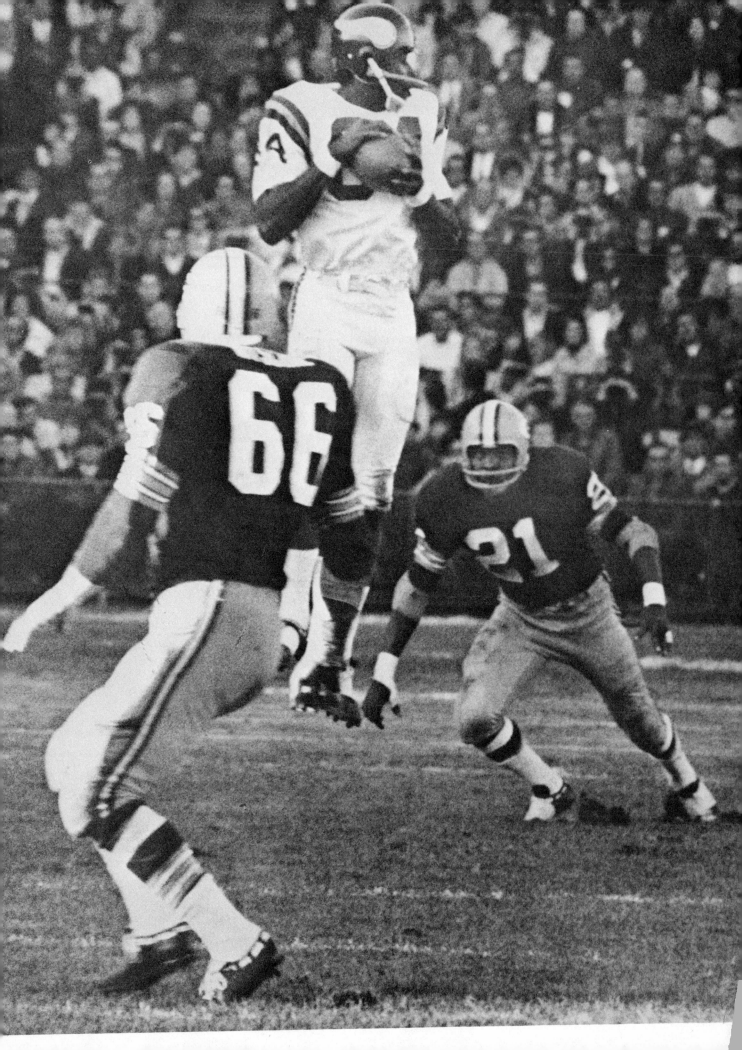

"As a pass receiver, Gene Washington is a quarterback's dream," said Joe Kapp of this great wide receiver.

The answer came when he became the starting tight end as a sophomore at Michigan State, besting a white candidate for the position. Now the question is academic.

A number-one draft choice of the Vikings in 1967, after breaking most of Michigan State's pass-catching records and becoming an All-American, Washington hoped and expected to start for Minnesota as a rookie. That was before he learned how Bud Grant felt about starting rookies. Instead, Washington backed up veteran Paul Flatley and caught only thirteen passes all season. However, they were good for 384 yards, a league-leading average of 29.5 yards per catch.

In 1968, "200 percent improved over the year before," according to Coach Grant, Washington caught forty-five passes for 756 yards and six touchdowns. This for a team ranking then next-to-last in passing in the then sixteen-team NFL with 1,995 total yards. Despite double-teaming, he grabbed thirty-nine passes for 821 yards and nine touchdowns in 1969, and caught forty-four for 702 yards and four scores in 1970. A painful injury to his foot limited him to twelve receptions for 165 yards in 1971. The acquisition of John Gilliam, plus periodic recurrences of his injury, resulted in eighteen catches for 259 yards and two touchdowns in 1972. Washington is too young and too talented not to regain his former eminence when his foot is fully healed. He and Gilliam will then give the Vikings real lightning at both wide receiver positions.

A magnificent all-around athlete, Washington uses many different skills to aid him in catching a football. "What I can do as a receiver goes back to what I've been able to do in other sports," he says. "In baseball, I played centerfield, so I know how to go deep for a ball over my head. In basketball, even when I was six-foot-two in high school, I could always dunk the ball. So I have always had jumping ability. In track, I had speed. And from playing tight end, I got the ruggedness to take the pounding a receiver has to take.

"The big thing, though, is that I've got this determination to win. And I think mainly it goes back to wanting to prove I wasn't just an all-black champion back in Texas."

Wide receiver John Gilliam (42) looks for a man to block as Clint Jones (26) runs with the ball.

john
gilliam

Memo to NFL cornerbacks: Do not attempt to psyche wide receiver John Gilliam by telling him he can't do something. Gilliam is a mean dude when challenged.

He was a happy basketball star at Brewer High School in Greenwood, South Carolina, when some classmates teased him about being afraid to play football. In his senior year he asked the coach if he could try out for the team. The coach thought he was kidding.

As Gilliam recalls it, "I asked again and he saw I was serious. The first workout he made me go one-on-one with the biggest tackle on the team. Blood was pumping from my nose and mouth. I felt like quitting, but I knew I couldn't take the teasing so I stuck it out. I made the starting team and was named the most outstanding player after the season."

The Viking offensive line is motionless as they await the signals from Fran Tarkenton, while the Pittsburgh defense carefully watches.

Apparently he's lived happily ever since in his new-found sport. He was an all-conference selection for three years at South Carolina State—at end as a sophomore, at flanker as a junior and at halfback as a senior. A second-round draft choice in the New Orleans Saints' first year of 1967, he and his team were off to a booming pro career on the first play of the season. He returned the kickoff ninety-four yards for a touchdown. The ball he carried is now in pro football's Hall of Fame in Canton, Ohio.

Gilliam saw part-time service as a runner and receiver in New Orleans, catching twenty-two and twenty-four passes in his two seasons before being traded to St. Louis for three players and a draft choice before the start of the 1969 season. Using his 9.4 speed, he caught 139 passes in three seasons with St. Louis, averaging twenty yards per reception, and scored seventeen touchdowns. On April 26, 1972, he was traded to the Vikings for Cuozzo and two draft choices. In his first season with Minnesota, he led the club in receiving by a wide margin, catching forty-seven passes for 1,035 yards, and making seven touchdowns.

Considering the Vikings' woes in the area of offensive running in 1972, Gilliam was a godsend to Tarkenton. Even before training camp Fran learned he could rely on the fleet receiver. Since Fran and Gilliam live in Atlanta in the off-season, they got acquainted with each other. After throwing to Gilliam for four days, the veteran quarterback raved about him. "His speed is fantastic and he is a super player . . . he knows how to run patterns. He is as well-conditioned an athlete as I've seen for a long time."

Jack Faulkner, the Saints' scout, wasn't surprised at Tarkenton's reaction. "I personally timed Gilliam in the 100-yard dash, and he ran 9.4, which is as fast as anybody runs in the NFL outside of Bob Hayes of Dallas. He has also run 4.5 in the 40-yard dash in full uniform . . . John is one of the receivers who can run all day. With Tarkenton at quarterback you can rest assured that he will hit Gilliam on some long bombs."

Rest assured. He did.

mick tingelhoff

Center Mick Tingelhoff: "Looking back, I have no regrets."

In 1955, when he was an 180-pound high-school sophomore in Lexington, Nebraska, Mick Tingelhoff's football position was permanently established. "The coach told me, 'We need a center. You're it,' " Tingelhoff recalls. "I've been a center ever since, although I also played defensive linebacker for a bit in college."

Centers are football's unknown soldiers. "Nobody really pays much attention to centers," Tingelhoff states. "You go around asking fans to name five starting centers on pro teams and how many can? They know the quarterbacks, the running backs, even the flankers and split ends. But centers? No Sir.

"But you know how it is with centers. They've got this helmet on, and their head always stuck down between their legs. They're always crouching over the ball or are buried under a pile of bodies. I remember when I first broke in, the only center who got any recognition at all was Jim Ringo, who had a consecutive game streak going at Green Bay."

As it turned out, Tingelhoff replaced Ringo as football's recognizable center for the same reason. The six-foot-two, 235-pound Viking is an outstanding ballplayer. Chosen All-Pro seven times and voted the NFL's top blocker in 1969, through the 1972 season he had played in 154 consecutive regular-season games. "When it comes time to pick the All-Pro team," he says with a smile, "the players or whoever else sits down to make the choices say, 'Center? Let's see now. There's Tingelhoff and . . .' They wrack their brains trying to think of who else plays center, then they say, 'Okay, it's Tingelhoff.' And that's how I'm All-Pro."

Not quite. You can be sure there are middle linebackers and safeties all over the league who, at one time or another, tried to blitz against the Vikings and got to know Tingelhoff intimately. He also calls blocking

an Tarkenton is about to take a snap
om seven-time All-Pro center Mick Tin-
lhoff.

changes at the line of scrimmage and centers for punts and field goals. Skill is involved. On field-goal tries the ball must come back to the holder with the laces facing the goal posts.

Tingelhoff has snapped the ball to several quarterbacks through the years—Kapp, Cuozzo, Lee and Tarkenton—and easily adjusted to the requirements of each.

"I can tell by the position of their hands just before the snap who is quarterbacking," Tingelhoff says. "The snap has to be one quick, cohesive movement. It's split-second timing, or else the play is busted or the quarterback fumbles. Coming off the snap quickly is another big thing. I try not to hesitate one bit after making the snap. Even a second of hesitation can enable a defensive lineman to break through and nail someone."

Although a Viking institution today, Tingelhoff was not pursued by Minnesota when he was a senior at the University of Nebraska in 1962. He wasn't pursued by anyone in either the NFL or AFL. Ignored by the draft, he signed as a free agent with the Vikings afterward.

How could a future All-Pro be so ignored by both leagues? "We didn't have very good teams at Nebraska during my time there," he explains. "We won only ten games in three years and none of the seniors on the 1961 club were drafted.

"I think the scouting today has become more sophisticated. There isn't as much chance of a major college player being overlooked. Just before the draft, St. Louis told me they were going to draft me. And Harry Gilmer, then assistant coach with the Vikings, had seen me on films and said Minnesota was going to take me.

"Imagine my surprise the day after the draft when my name wasn't mentioned in the newspapers. St. Louis and the Vikings then offered me contracts as a free agent, and I picked the Vikings because they were a young club and I figured I'd have a better chance of making the team. That was a long time ago and, looking back, I have no regrets. And as a free agent I was able to get a better contract than some of the fellows who were drafted."

Amazingly, he wound up being better-known than they.